Victory Over Anger:
Rules of Engagement

Workbook

By Dr. Teresa Davis, Ed.D.

The purpose of this workbook is to help you the reader not only recognize your anger, but also to help you work through it, to help you apply the techniques discussed in the book, and to help you learn better methods to handle your anger in appropriate ways.

This workbook works in conjunction with the book of the same title. Each chapter of the book has a corresponding chapter in the workbook. It is suggested that you read through the book itself at least once. Then set aside 17 weeks to work through the book and workbook together. You might want to read the corresponding chapter several times during that week. Be sure to spend some time in prayer before and during the time you are working through this workbook. Ask God to show you the changes He wants you to make, then show you how to make them. God will faithfully show you what will work best for you. It is His will for you to handle your anger in a Godly way.

If you are a person who struggles with extreme outbursts of anger, deep rooted anger, domestic violence, and/or are abusive in any way to others, it is HIGHLY suggested you seek out professional help while, and in addition to working through these books.

Suggested web sites for finding Christian Counselors in your area:
Focus on the Family - www.family.org
American Association of Christian Counselors - www.aacc.net

For questions, suggestions, or comments about this book or workbook, please email me at drteresadavis@cox.net.

Thanks,
Teresa Davis <><
Merry Heart Ministries

Introduction

1. Read chapter
2. Complete anger checklist
3. Look up the words nature and nurture in a dictionary (and/or other reference books) and develop your own definition.
4. Considering both nurture (what you are taught) and nature (what you inherit, biological) fill out worksheet #1.
5. Find a story in a magazine or newspaper that tells about something that happened as a result of anger. Write a brief description of the article and give details about the person involved anger issues. Based on what you know about them, write what you think their home life could have been like. Add your ideas about the nature/nurture issue. Answer the following questions:
    a. Was it hard or easy for you to imagine this person's home life?
    b. Did you relate it to your own experiences or to those of someone you know?
    c. Did you think of an alternate way they could have responded to the situation?

Anger Checklist
(Pre-test and Post-test)

This test is a method of assessing your level of anger. Everyone will recognize some of these characteristics so don't worry - be honest. When answering the following questions, think about your behavior in terms of the last two to three months.

never 1 2 3 4 5 always

1. I can handle difficult or demanding projects without getting upset............................1 2 3 4 5

2. I feel the need to defend myself..1 2 3 4 5

3. I feel threatened if someone else is being complimented...1 2 3 4 5

4. I try to act instead of react in difficult situations..1 2 3 4 5

5. I withdraw when I am upset or angry...1 2 3 4 5

6. I think in advance about what I will do if someone hurts or offends me....................1 2 3 4 5

7. I have a positive outlook about others...1 2 3 4 5

8. I feel the need to be perfect..1 2 3 4 5

9. I can forgive and forget when others hurt or offend me..1 2 3 4 5

10. I take my personal frustrations out on others...1 2 3 4 5

11. I avoid seeing others with whom I have had difficulties with....................................1 2 3 4 5

12. When I am trying to prove my point, my tone of voice is likely
    to become louder...1 2 3 4 5

13. I get angry with others who refuse to admit their weaknesses.................................1 2 3 4 5

14. I welcome opposing viewpoints...1 2 3 4 5

15. I feel annoyed when others do not understand my needs...1 2 3 4 5

16. I keep my emotions under control..1 2 3 4 5

17. Disappointments cause me to want to quit...1 2 3 4 5

18. I like to win at playing games, even when it is just for fun.......................................1 2 3 4 5

19. I can be aggressive...1 2 3 4 5

20. I feel frustrated when I see someone else having fewer struggles than I do...........1 2 3 4 5

21. Life treats me fair...1 2 3 4 5

22. I blame others for my problems..1 2 3 4 5

23. I find myself being impatient..1 2 3 4 5

24. I say careless things that are hurtful to others..................................1 2 3 4 5

25. I hide my true feelings by acting nice to people who I am irritated at......1 2 3 4 5

26. I get defensive when others are annoyed with me...........................1 2 3 4 5

27. I feel depressed or discouraged...1 2 3 4 5

28. When I get upset I drink alcohol or use drugs..................................1 2 3 4 5

29. I nurture critical thoughts..1 2 3 4 5

30. I am offended with even constructive criticism.................................1 2 3 4 5

31. I feel the need to prove myself when I think I am right......................1 2 3 4 5

32. When conversing with others, I am thinking of my rebuttal
    as he or she speaks..1 2 3 4 5

33. I try to control others...1 2 3 4 5

34. I have difficulty falling or staying asleep..1 2 3 4 5

35. I am physically sick or don't feel well...1 2 3 4 5

36. People like to be around me...1 2 3 4 5

37. I find myself doing or saying things I need to apologizing for............1 2 3 4 5

38. I walk away from possible fights or disagreements...........................1 2 3 4 5

39. I can accept my own mistake...1 2 3 4 5

40. I will argue a point if I feel I am right..1 2 3 4 5

41. I enjoy life..1 2 3 4 5

42. I find myself disappointed because I have not reached my goals.......1 2 3 4 5

43. I fear what others may think of me..1 2 3 4 5

44. I fret over how I will manage important events..................................1 2 3 4 5

45. Others tell me I need to calm down...1 2 3 4 5

46. I feel tense..1 2 3 4 5

47. I yell or scream when I get angry..1 2 3 4 5

48. I enjoy life's ups and downs...1 2 3 4 5

49. I worry..1 2 3 4 5

50. I try to live up to other's expectations of me..1 2 3 4 5

Add your total scores using the numbers you circled except for questions 1, 4, 7, 9, 14, 16, 21, 36, 38, 39, 41, & 48. Reverse the scores on these questions; if you circled 5, your score will be 1, 4 = 2, 3 = 3, 2 = 4, 1 = 5.

50-125   People who score in this range usually have a high tolerance for anger.

125-175   People who score in this range tend to be easily angered.

175 - 250   People who score in this range are dealing with extreme anger.

Introduction
Worksheet #1
Anger History

In the space below, write a fairly detailed history of your family of origin and how anger was displayed in your home. If you were not raised by your biological parents, give a discription of what you know about them, then describe the home you were raised in. Include details about siblings. Discuss how you feel nature and nurture played a role in the way you currently display anger. Also, discuss any other life experiences you think may have played a role in this matter (i.e. death of a loved one, an accident, abuse, handicap, etc. . .). Use an extra sheet of paper if you need more room.

_____

_____

_____

_____

_____

_____

_____

_____

_____

_____

_____

_____

_____

_____

_____

Chapter 1
Anger Is A Choice

1. Read chapter.
2. Fill out worksheet #2
3. Identifying what changes your body makes when you become angry is essential in anger management. Fill out worksheet #3.

Chapter 1
Worksheet #2
Anger Choices

Use a thesaurus, synonyms, antonyms, homonyms and/or dictionary, and develop your own definition for the following words:

1. Anger_____

_____

_____

2. Choice_____

_____

_____

3. What are the things we usually don't have a choice about? _____

_____

_____

4. What type things do we have a choice about? _____

_____

_____

_____

5. Besides the ones listed in the chapter, find and write out several additional scriptures from the Bible that mentions anger. You can also include words such as self-control and rage. _____

_____

_____

_____

_____

6. Re-word at least one of the scriptures you listed so that it applies to you personally. _____

_____

_____

_____

_____

7. List 10 motives for **your** anger (i.e. abuse, injustice, ignorance, manipulation)

1. _____

2. _____

3. _____

4. _____

5. _____

6. _____

7. _____

8. _____

9. _____

10. _____

8. Pick 5 of the above motives and write I statements about how you feel when these things happen.

1. _____

2. _____

3. _____

4. _____

5. _____

Chapter 1
Worksheet #3
Identifying Effects

1. Briefly describe the most recent time that you displayed anger in an inappropriate way and later suffered severe consequences as a result.

_____

_____

_____

_____

2. Using the above example, try to remember how you acted when you got angry.

   Check all the responses that apply to you.

   _____ yelled and/or screamed   _____ hit something

   _____ stomped out   _____ held in your anger
                                                  (stuffed)
   _____ drank alcohol   _____ used drugs

   _____ cried   _____ got angry at yourself

   _____ slammed doors   _____ hit someone

   _____ took the anger out on someone or something other than what you were
          actually angry about (scapegoating).

3. See if you can remember how your body felt when you became angry.

   Sometimes it helps to close your eyes and visualize the incident.

   _____ sweaty palms   _____ grit your teeth

   _____ stomach muscles tightened   _____ heart pound

   _____ dizziness   _____ feel heat in your face

   _____ get shaky   _____ head spin or pound

   _____ other   _____ other

Chapter 2
Self-Talk

1. Read chapter.
2. Fill out worksheet #4.
3. Realizing that there is always more than one perspective in any given situation can change the way you view difficult situations you encounter in life. We will focus on other's perspectives several times throughout this workbook, so we can learn to push ourselves to see the other side(s) of a situation. Go to a public place with a lot of people (i.e. zoo, shopping mall, movie theater). Observe several sets, or groups, of people for about 30 minutes. Then pick what you think is the most impressive incident between people that you saw happening. See if you can imagine both (or more) of the perspectives that were present in this situation. Write a brief summary of the situation and your conclusions.
4. Fill out worksheet #5. You will need to make several copies of this worksheet before filling it out because you will be assigned it every week through the end of this study. You can copy it single or double sided, depending if you think you will need the extra space on back for writing.

Chapter 2
Worksheet #4
Using Self-Talk

1. Utilizing self-talk can help us get out of some pretty sticky situations. Using the space below, develop your own scenario of an angry situation. Then, self-talk your way through this situation. You can use a made up scenario, or one from your own life. _____

    _____

    _____

    _____

    _____

    _____

    _____

    _____

2. Now write out at least 5 scriptures you could use to help you through this situation. _____

    _____

    _____

    _____

3. Think of a time you have gotten offended by someone close to you and write it below. _____

    _____

    _____

    _____

4. How could you have used self-talk with, or without, scriptures to get yourself through this same situation without getting offended? _____

_____

_____

_____

_____

5. In a car wreck, there are at least 2 drivers involved. Give 2 possible perspectives to this car wreck, each from one of the people involved. Describe how each could affect their lives differently (remember that your perspective is your reality).

Driver 1 _____

_____

_____

_____

Driver 2 _____

_____

_____

_____

6. How do you think perspective can be different from fact? Give an example.

_____

_____

_____

_____

_____

_____

Chapter 2
Worksheet #5
Anger Log

You will need to make several copies of this worksheet because you will be filling one out once a week from now until the end of this class. This will help you see how well you are applying the principles taught. You will fill this out based on situations where you find yourself angry. It should be done after the incident is over.

1.   What is the situation? _____

_____

_____

_____

_____

2.   Who is involved? _____

_____

3.   How did you respond? _____

_____

_____

_____

_____

4.   Was this a typical response for you? If no, explain. _____

_____

_____

_____

5.   On a scale of 1 to 10, with one being the best and 10 being the worse, how do you feel you controlled your anger? (Remember, stuffing or withdrawing is not appropriate.)_____

6.   What was the outcome or consequence? _____

_____

_____

_____

7.   Is this the result you were looking for? Why or why not? _____

_____

_____

_____

8.   How could you have responded differently? _____

_____

_____

_____

9.   Write out several Bible verses that talk about this type situation. _____

_____

_____

_____

10.   How do you feel about this situation now? _____

_____

_____

_____

Chapter 3
Our Thought Process

1. Read chapter.
2. Fill out worksheet #6
3. Fill out worksheet #5
4. Think of a recent situation you experienced (car wreck, disagreement, loss of job, etc...). Write out the positives and negatives of that situation. Include what you heard and watched in that situation (verbal and non-verbal).

Chapter 3
Worksheet #6
Our Thought Process

1. Are you dealing with something right now that the enemy keeps telling you negative things about? Describe the situation. _____

    _____

    _____

    _____

    _____

2. List the negative thoughts. _____

    _____

    _____

    _____

    _____

3. Name several things you can think about in place of the negative thoughts.

    _____

    _____

    _____

    _____

4. Find several positive messages in the Bible and write them below.

    _____

    _____

    _____

    _____

    _____

5.   What is the difference between negative thoughts and worry? _____

_____

_____

_____

6.   Name the things you consistently worry about (i.e. job, money, kids, spouse). Be
      specifics. _____

_____

_____

_____

7.   What good things can you think about instead of worrying? _____

_____

_____

_____

8.   Who is the first person you think about telling when something good, scary,
      exciting, etc. . . happens in your life? _____

9.   Is this person someone who confronts you with truth, or are they someone who
      joins your 'pity party?" _____

10.   List those people you know you can call that will join your pity party. _____

_____

_____

_____

11.   List those people you know who will confront you and be honest with you.

_____

_____

_____

12. Name something you are really good at. How often did you/do you practice?

_____

_____

13. List your habits, positive and negative. _____

_____

_____

_____

_____

_____

14. Have you ever tried to break a habit? Pick one of the negative habits you listed

and briefly outline how you would try to break it. _____

_____

_____

_____

15. Think of a new, positive habit you would like to start. Outline how you will go

about making this a habit. Do you think it is true that after you do the same thing

for 21 days it becomes a habit? _____

_____

_____

_____

(We will again address the issue of habits when we discuss the chapter on goal setting.)

Chapter 4
Emotions and Anger

1. Read chapter.
2. Write out your answer to the following question: Why do you think we live in such an angry world?
3. Fill out worksheet #7
4. Fill out worksheet #5
5. Read over "12 Tips For Tough Times." Copy and/or reduce, or write it out on index cards so you can keep it with you for a reminder.
6. Watching other people you are around (or movies, TV, sports, etc. . .), see if you can recognize emotions stuffed and expressed as anger. Write a brief summary of what you observe.
7. Fill out worksheet #8

Chapter 4
Worksheet #7
Emotions and Anger

1. How do you express your anger? _____

    _____

    _____

    _____

2. My husband told me once that he felt like he had to walk around on eggshells wondering what I was going to blow up about next. How do you think your family and friends feel about the way you express your anger? _____

    _____

    _____

    _____

3. Think of a recent time when you expressed anger instead of another emotion. Briefly describe. _____

    _____

    _____

4. What emotion did you stuff in that situation? _____

5. How could you have handled this situation differently by expressing the true emotion? _____

    _____

    _____

6. Using the attached Emotional Faces Chart, circle the emotions you think you consistently show anger in place of.

7. Using a separate piece of paper, list the things from your past that you have not emotionally dealt with but know you need to. Depending on the magnitude of the different situations, think of some ways you can begin to deal with them (i.e. prayer, counseling, journaling, talking to a friend, etc. . .).

 EXHAUSTED
 CONFUSED
 ECSTATIC
 GUILTY
 SUSPICIOUS

 ANGRY
 HYSTERICAL
 FRUSTRATED
 SAD
 CONFIDENT

 EMBARRASSED
 HAPPY
 MISCHIEVOUS
 DISGUSTED
 FRIGHTENED

 ENRAGED
 ASHAMED
 CAUTIOUS
 SMUG
 DEPRESSED

 OVERWHELMED
 HOPEFUL
 LONELY
 LOVESTRUCK
 JEALOUS

 BORED
 SURPRISED
 ANXIOUS
 SHOCKED
 SHY

12 TIPS FOR TOUGH TIMES

Both research and experience show that when people with anger problems change their self-talk, their anger de-escalates and they regain control. When you feel yourself starting to get angry, take a TIME-OUT and read these statements to yourself. Transfer them to 3 X 5 note cards, and read them several times a day as well as during your time-outs.

- I don't need to prove myself in this situation. I can stay calm.

- As long as I keep my cool, I'm in control of myself.

- No need to doubt myself—what other people say doesn't matter. I'm the only person who can make me mad or keep me calm.

- Time to relax and slow things down. Take a time-out if I get tight.

- My anger is a signal. Time to talk to myself and to relax.

- I don't need to feel threatened here. I can relax and stay cool.

- Nothing says I have to be competent and strong all the time. It's OK to feel unsure or confused.

- It is impossible to control other people and situations. The only thing I can control is myself and how I express my feelings.

- It is OK to be uncertain or insecure sometimes. I don't need to be in control of everything and everybody.

- If people criticize me, I can survive that. Nothing says I have to be perfect.

- If this person wants to go off the wall, that's their thing. I don't need to respond to their anger or feel threatened.

- When I get into an argument, I can stay with my plan and know what to do. I can take a time-out.

- Most things we argue about are stupid and insignificant. I can recognize that my anger is just my old primary feelings being re-stimulated. It is OK to walk away from this fight.

- It is nice to have other people's love and approval, but even without it, I can still accept and like myself.

- People put erasers on the ends of pencils for a reason. It is OK to make mistakes.

- People are going to act the way they want to, not the way I want.

- I feel angry. That must mean I have been hurt or scared.

If you have trouble answering some of these questions, refer back to the Faces page.

1.   When I am angry I feel _____

2.   When things don't go my way I feel _____

3.   When someone close to me is hurting I feel _____

4.   When someone does something nice to or for me I feel _____

5.   When someone does something bad or negative to me I feel _____

6.   When I feel I have done something wrong I feel _____

7.   When someone criticizes me I feel _____

8.   When I lose something I feel _____

9.   When someone 'road rages' around me I feel _____

10.   When someone shows their anger around me I feel _____

11.   When someone directs their anger at me I feel _____

12.   When I find out something I shouldn't know I feel _____

13.   When I find out someone has kept a secret from me I feel _____

14.   When I think someone is talking about me in a negative way I feel _____

15.   When someone tells me 'no' I feel _____

16.   When I am not included in an invitation where I know others are, (i.e. lunch,

      party, etc. . .) I feel _____

17.   When I do something stupid I feel _____

18.   When I don't get what I think I deserve (i.e. job, raise, blessing, etc. . .) I feel

      _____

19. When it seems others are more blessed than me I feel _____

20. When I am alone I feel _____

21. When I am in a crowd I feel _____

22. When I have a good day I feel _____

23. When things seem to pile up all around me I feel _____

24. When I am around important people I feel _____

25. When others get what I think I should have gotten I feel _____

26. When I am in situations that I have no control over I feel _____

27. When I am in messy or dirty places I feel _____

28. When I know I need to be doing something but I am not I feel _____

29. When I am called on to speak in public I feel _____

30. When I am around chaos I feel _____

Chapter 5
Rejection

1. Read Chapter
2. Fill out worksheet #5
3. Fill out worksheet #9
4. Fill out worksheet # 10
5. Watching a movie or TV show, find a character who, during the show, is rejected in some way. On a piece of notebook paper, describe the situation and what you think they may feel. Then answer the following questions. How did they act as a result? Did they confront the situation or try to cover it up? What would you have said to this person if you were there? What would you have done if this were you? Would your reaction have been appropriate? What do you think would have been the most appropriate thing to do in this situation?

Chapter 5
Worksheet #9
Rejection

1. Identify a time when you have felt rejected. _____

_____

_____

2. How did you feel? _____

3. How did you act? _____

4. What emotion did you actually display? _____

5. What is your normal reaction to feelings of rejection? _____

_____

_____

6. There are several reasons mentioned in the text that natural rejection occurs. Do you fit into any of those categories? If yes, which one(s)? _____

_____

_____

7. Do you think you suffer with an overall fear of rejection as a result? _____

8. What do you do to prevent feeling rejected? _____

_____

_____

_____

9. On a separate piece of paper try to describe the "yous" of your personality; who you are behind the different masks you wear. Be as detailed as possible. Explain why you act differently around different people. Try to identify which of the masks is closest to being the "real" you. Who do you feel the "safest" being around? What can you do to try to be the same person no matter what circumstances you are in? Be sure to include the situations where you display anger in its' truest form – for you. Be honest.

Chapter 5
Worksheet #10
Recognizing Your Strengths

Most of us have been told all our lives to not "brag" about ourselves. If we do, we sound arrogant, big headed, or vain. As a result, we don't recognize anything positive about ourselves, but we believe and confess the negative things we have been told, and that's okay. The Bible tells us to "Love our neighbors as ourselves" (Matthew 19:19). How can we do this if we won't even recognize the good things about ourselves? This worksheet will help you to recognize some of the areas where you are the strongest. For some of you, this worksheet will be very difficult because you have never admitted to yourself, much less others, anything that you are good at. You may feel embarrassed to write your answers. Do it anyways. This will be very good for your self-esteem and your self-confidence. It will also help you to begin to feel better about who you are. Try to answer each questions with a different answer. If you have too hard of a time coming up with different answers, ask someone you are close to and trust to help you. These answers can vary from the simple, such as housecleaning or cooking, to the complex, such as singing or playing a musical instrument.

1.   I am really good at _____

2.   I really enjoy doing _____

3.   Others say I am good at _____

4.   _____ is my greatest accomplishment.

5.   I have pretty/nice looking _____

6.   I look the best when I _____

7.   I feel the best when I _____

8.   Other people like me because _____

9.   Other people say I have great looking _____

10.   People ask me to _____

11.   My best friend is _____

12.   He/she likes me because _____

13.   The person that knows me best is _____

14.   He/she would tell you that I am _____

15. The person who helps me feel good about myself is _____

Because _____

_____

_____

_____

16. Try to think of yourself the way someone else does, based on what they have said to you in the past. Now describe yourself. Be specific. If you need to, ask someone you trust for help. _____

_____

_____

_____

_____

_____

_____

_____

_____

_____

_____

_____

_____

_____

Chapter 6
Unrealistic Expectations

1. Read chapter.
2. Fill out worksheet #5
3. Fill out worksheet #11
4. Have someone you trust fill out worksheet #12 for you.
5. Think of a time in your life when you have had a difficult situation arise as a result of unrealistic expectations (several examples are given in the chapter). Briefly summarize. Explain all the unrealistic expectations you can think of including "shoulds" and "needs." Next, develop a more realistic way to handle that situation.

Chapter 6
Worksheet #11
Unrealistic Expectations

1. Using a dictionary, define "unrealistic." _____

   _____

   _____

2. Define "expectations." _____

   _____

   _____

3. Using the definitions you wrote from the dictionary, develop your own definition for "unrealistic expectations." _____

   _____

   _____

4. Based on that definition, briefly summarize a couple of areas where you may have unrealistic expectations on yourself. Consider the words "should" and "need" that you may consciously or subconsciously say to yourself.

   _____

   _____

   _____

   _____

5. Why do you think you have those expectations? Thinking about your past, how do you think those expectations developed? _____

   _____

   _____

   _____

   _____

   _____

6.   Now do the same thing with unrealistic expectations you have on others (i.e. A clean house should be important to her.) _____

_____

_____

_____

_____

7.   Why do you think you have those expectations? Thinking about your past, how do you think those expectations developed? (i.e. You grew up in a really dirty house and now a clean one is really important to you) _____

_____

_____

_____

_____

8.   On a separate piece of paper, discuss the differences in backgrounds between you and someone you are close to, like a close friend or a spouse. Be specific. How were you raised? What kind of lifestyle did you live? How were you disciplined? Did you do things together as a family? Did you do chores? Did you have boundaries and how were those boundaries different? Were you given allowance and how were you allowed to spend it? Were you raised in church? Were you raised in a Christian home? Think of and answer as many of these types of questions as can.

9.   Identify where these differences can, or have, caused conflict in your relationship with this person. _____

_____

_____

10. How do you feel when someone is placing expectations on you that you either don't feel like you can do, or you don't necessarily want to do? _____

_____

.

11. Who or what do you tend to compare your life to? (i.e. others, TV shows, movies, etc...) _____

_____

_____

_____

12. How do you think you compare to them? _____

_____

13. Why do you think you compare to them specifically? _____

_____

14. In the text, Tony had very unrealistic expectations about how his home would be when he got there. Write a realistic view of your life (the way it really is, not the way you wish it was). _____

_____

_____

_____

_____

_____

15. Is it okay for your life to be the way it is right now? _____

16. If the answer to #15 is no, list a few goals you could work towards in an effort to change things. Try to think of them from a viewpoint of preventing panic, feelings of failure, explosions, and disappointments. (Refer to the ones mentioned for Tony in the text if you need help) _____

_____

_____

_____

_____

17.   Think of a time you have felt like you have failed at something. _____

_____

_____

_____

18.   From the perspective of "hindsight is 20/20," did you set yourself up for failure? What are some ways you could have prevented this situation from ending in failure? _____

_____

_____

_____

19.   Do you know anyone who has lost everything they has as a result of a mid-life crisis (or something similar)? What happened? Thinking back, identify where you think the problems might have started. Can you think of ways this person could have prevented this from happening? How? _____

_____

_____

_____

Worksheet #12
How others feel about me.

Student: Have someone you are close to and trust fill this worksheet out for you.
Friend: Please fill this out as honestly as possible for me and answer each question with a different response.

(Student's name) _____

Loves to _____

Is fun to _____

Is really good at _____

Has great _____

Greatest strength is _____

Looks the best when _____

Handles difficult situations by _____

Brings out _____ me.

I like spending time with him/her because _____

_____

The thing I most appreciate about him/her is _____

_____

I can always rely on him/her for _____

_____

He/she has helped me the most by _____

_____

_____

Additional Comments: _____

_____

_____

_____

Chapter 7

We Want Our Way

1. Read chapter.
2. Fill out worksheet #5
3. Read information about the Johari Window on the following pages and fill out your personal window. On the back of that same sheet, describe how you feel about yourself after viewing the information you filled in.
4. Fill out worksheet #13

Johari Window

The Johari Window can provide a way for us to see not only how we view ourselves, but also how others view us. In relationships, the more we trust a person, the more comfortable we will be to share details about our lives with them. People sometimes notice things about us that we are not aware of. Sometimes it takes several people several times of telling us something is true about ourselves before we believe it to be true. Isn't it funny how the negative things people say about us are so easy to believe, but it is very difficult to believe the positive? Hopefully, this exercise will help you to have a better understanding about who you are, based on the truths you know about yourself (but sometimes are unwilling to admit) and what others see in you.

Joe Luft and Harry Ingham were researching human personality at the University of California in the 1950's when they devised their Johari Window. Using a form of word derivation normally reserved for suburban house names, they based the title on their two first names. They observed that there are aspects of our personality that we're open about, and other elements that we keep to ourselves. At the same time, there are things that others see in us that we're not aware of. As a result, you can draw up a four-box grid, which includes a fourth group of traits that are unknown to anyone:

Area 2 This area is known to others but not to me	**Area 3** This area is unknown to me and to others
Area 1 This area is known to both me and others	**Area 4** This area is known to me but not to others.

Area 1 contains things that are openly known and talked about - and which may be seen as strengths or weaknesses. This is the self that others observe and we choose to share with others. This will include things such as race, name, height, weight, etc... as well as things you have chosen to share. Usually, the more you get to know people, the freer you will feel about sharing personal things.

Area 2 contains things that others observe that we don't know about. Again, they could be positive or negative behaviors, and will affect the way that others act towards us. An example would be the woman who tells her husband he snores at night? He didn't think he did, but she knew he did.

Area 3 contains things that nobody knows about us - including ourselves. This may be because we've never exposed those areas of our personality, or because they're buried deep in the subconscious.

Area 4 contains aspects of our self that we know about and keep hidden from others. It contains all the information that we don't want others to know about us. It's that closet of feelings, insecurities, and not-so-great experiences. It is the private information.

with thanks to John Morris

A change in any of the four areas will affect other areas. An example is, as we share more about ourselves, Area 4 will become smaller and Area 1 will become larger. As God reveals things to us, maybe things He wants us to work on changing, Area 3 will become smaller which will affect Areas 1 and 4, depending on how much we choose to disclose about that situation to others.

This Johari Window information was complied using information from these two websites: http://www.chimaeraconsulting.com/johari.htm   http://cls.coe.utk.edu/pdf/ls/Week2_Lesson12.pdf

Your Personal Johari Window

Understanding how you view yourself, and the way others see you, will help you have a better perspective of who you really are. Using worksheets #10 and #12 fill in the boxes accordingly. You may want to add in other things that you feel would fit that aren't necessarily part of either worksheet.

Known to others, but not me	Not known to me or others

Known to me and others	Known to me, but not to others

Chapter 7
Worksheet #13
We Want Our Way

1.   List the top 5 things you get angry about.
     a. _____

     b. _____

     c. _____

     d. _____

     e. _____

2.   Identify what it is about each situation you listed above that you are wanting your way about (even if it is justified).
     a. _____

     b. _____

     c. _____

     d. _____

     e. _____

3.   For each of these situations, think of an alternative plan of how to handle them in an appropriate way without losing control.
     a. _____

     b. _____

     c. _____

     d. _____

     e. _____

4.   Give the first name of someone you are currently angry with. _____

5.   Briefly describe the reason. _____

_____

_____

6.   Does the other person know you are angry at them? _____

7.   If yes, what is/was their response? _____

_____

_____

8.   Many times the people we are angry with go on with their lives forgetting the situation, while we are consumed by it. When this happens, we are allowing that person to control our feelings. List some ways you can get over the anger you have about this situation (hint: you may want to consider forgiveness, even if they don't deserve it). _____

_____

_____

_____

9.   Identify the times when you realize your stress level is higher than normal.

_____

_____

10. What are some things you can do to avoid confrontations during these times?

_____

_____

_____

11. List some areas that you normally get upset about, but may not be as important as you sometimes act like they are. _____

_____

_____

12. What can you do to change the way you act when these things happen? _____

_____

_____

Chapter 8
Act or React

1. Read chapter.
2. Fill out worksheet #5
3. Fill out worksheet #14

Chapter 8
Worksheet #14
Act or React

1.   Name something in your life you feel like you have accomplished. _____

_____

_____

2.   What steps did you go through in order to succeed at this accomplishment?

_____

_____

_____

_____

3.   How differently could this situation have turned out if you had not followed through with the steps you did? _____

_____

_____

4.   What is the first change you notice in your body when you become angry?
_____

5.   Is there any other times besides when you are angry that you feel the same body change? If yes, when? _____

_____

_____

6.   Name a time when you typically find yourself getting angry. This needs to be something that happens on a continuing bases (i.e. repeating yourself to you children). _____

_____

_____

7. Develop a plan of action to use the next time this same situation occurs which will help you maintain your control. Include the recognized body change.

_____

_____

_____

_____

_____

8. How do you feel after you have lost your temper or thrown a temper tantrum?

_____

_____

9. Describe how you justify your anger (i.e. It's the only way to get them to listen).

_____

_____

_____

10. How can you change justification to accountability and responsibility? _____

_____

_____

_____

_____

_____

11. How do you feel when you are around someone who is expressing their anger, both appropriately or inappropriately? _____

_____

_____

_____

12. How do you feel when you are around people who are arguing and/or fighting?

_____

_____

_____

13. How do you think others feel when they are around you and you are displaying your anger in inappropriate ways? _____

_____

_____

_____

14. Do you think your reactions to upsetting circumstances are appropriate (remember what scripture says about "not sinning"). Why or why not?

_____

_____

_____

15. How would you like to see yourself act? Do you think this is possible? Why or why not? _____

_____

_____

_____

Chapter 9
Are You Passive, Aggressive, or Assertive?

1. Read chapter.
2. Fill out worksheet #5 (Are you noticing any differences?)
3. Fill out worksheet # 15
4. Using the three scenarios listed below, write out how you think a passive, an aggressive, and an assertive person would handle each situation.

   Scenario #1   You are driving down the street and another car hits yours. It is their fault.

   Scenario #2   You purchased something from a department store they advertised on sale, but find out later the clerk charged you the regular price.

   Scenario #3   Your kid comes home from school with a note accusing him of doing something he says he didn't do.

Chapter 9
Worksheet #15
Are You Passive, Aggressive, or Assertive?

1. Do you tend to naturally be more passive or aggressive? Explain. _____

    _____

    _____

    _____

2. Briefly describe a recent time that you were extremely passive or aggressive.

    _____

    _____

    _____

    _____

3. How did you feel after this incident? _____

    _____

4. How did you self-talk? (i.e. I can't believe I just said yes when I wanted to say no
    – again). _____

    _____

    _____

    _____

5. After reading this chapter and doing the class exercise, describe how you could

    have handled that same situation in an assertive way. _____

    _____

    _____

    _____

    _____

6. Write out how you would say this. _____

_____

_____

7. Name someone who handles difficult or strained situations opposite of the way you do. _____

8. How do you feel about the way they handle things? _____

_____

_____

9. Why do you think you feel this way? _____

_____

_____

10. Name a situation where you would like to say *no*, but haven't been able to.

_____

_____

_____

11. Write out an appropriate assertive way to say *no* in this situation. _____

_____

_____

_____

Chapter 10
Seeing Other's Perspective

1. Read chapter.
2. Fill out worksheet #5
3. Fill out worksheet #16
4. Make a collage out of pictures of people cut from magazines and newspapers. Label each person's expression. Then using one or more of the pictures you have selected, develop your own paradigm shift story and briefly summarize.

Chapter 10
Seeing Others Perspective
Worksheet #16

1. Name several typical times you know when you get irritated. (i.e. slow lines, slow traffic, something rings up incorrectly at store). _____

_____

_____

2. For each of the things you listed above, write out an appropriate way to respond to them. _____

_____

_____

_____

_____

3. Write out imagined stories of what other people in these situations might be experiencing or what the cause might be. _____

_____

_____

_____

_____

4. Write out each of the scriptures listed below. Then write out how you feel about each of them and how easy or difficult they are to apply to your life.

1 Thess. 5:15 _____

_____

_____

_____

_____

Eph. 4:32 _____

_____

_____

_____

1 Pet. 3:8-9 _____

_____

_____

_____

_____

Prov. 15:1 _____

_____

_____

_____

Prov. 25:21-22 _____

_____

_____

_____

Matt: 7:12 _____

_____

_____

_____

Chapter 11
Goal Setting

1. Read chapter.
2. Fill out worksheet #5.
3. Fill out worksheet #17
4. Develop your own time line with short and long term goals and rewards for something you would like to accomplish.

Chapter 11
Worksheet #17
Goal Setting

1. Name something you have strived to accomplish but feel you failed. _____
   _____

2. Why do you think you failed? _____
   _____
   _____

3. How did you feel? _____
   _____

4. How do your feel about that situation now? _____
   _____

5. Do you feel like this is a pattern for you? Explain. _____
   _____

6. After reading this chapter, how do you think you could have changed the way you approached and accomplished this goal? _____
   _____
   _____
   _____

7. Name several ways you are hard on yourself. _____
   _____
   _____

8. How do you feel when others do the same things you mentioned in #7? _____
   _____
   _____

9. Do you give others a break, but not yourself? Explain and give examples.

_____

_____

10. List some things you could use as self-rewards when accomplishing small goals.

_____

_____

11. Name a time when you were working on or towards something that you "threw in the towel" after one, or a couple of bad days. _____

_____

12. How would you change that now? _____

_____

_____

13. Have you ever made a list of items you wanted to accomplish in a day? Explain.

_____

_____

14. How did it feel as you began completing the tasks on the list? _____

_____

15. Did you finish the list that day? Why or why not? _____

_____

_____

16. Did you feel better about what you did accomplish or worse about what you didn't accomplish? Explain. _____

_____

_____

Chapter 12
Are You Angry With God?

1.   Read chapter.
2.   Fill out worksheet #5
3.   Fill out worksheet #18
4.   Describe a trial you have went through in your past. List several things you recognize now, that you didn't see when you were going through the trial. These should be things that you now realize God was doing that you couldn't see then.

Chapter 12
Worksheet #18
Are You Angry With God?

1. What is the last major trial you remember going through? _____

    _____

    _____

2. How did you feel when you were going through this trial? _____

    _____

    _____

3. How do you think you handled it? _____

    _____

4. What did you/have you learned as a result of this trial? _____

    _____

    _____

    _____

5. When is the last time you remember being angry with God? _____

    _____

6. Why were you angry at him? _____

    _____

7. Were you honest with God about his? Why or why not? _____

    _____

    _____

8. How was this situation resolved? _____

    _____

9. What did you learn as a result of this situation? _____

_____

_____

10. Describe a time when God has used something you felt was negative in your life for yours or someone else's good? _____

_____

_____

11. Do you think what you went through was worth it? Why or why not? _____

_____

_____

12. Name a time where you recognize you went through a time of spiritual growth.

_____

_____

_____

13. What do you think caused the most growth? _____

_____

_____

14. Have you been able to help others who were going through the same 'type' of situations as a result of your growth? Explain. _____

_____

_____

15. Discuss "no pain, no gain," from the perspective of this situation. _____

_____

_____

16.	Describe a situation that you have had to endure several times (or similar situations like, financial struggles). _____

_____

17.	What do you think the Lord is wanting you to learn through these type situations?

_____

_____

_____

18.	What do you think is your weakest "spiritual" area? _____

_____

_____

19.	Is this an area where you feel the enemy continues to attack? Why or why not?

_____

_____

20.	What do you think you are going to have to change, learn, or do, in order to overcome these attacks? _____

_____

_____

21.	Discuss the scripture that talks about Christ being strong in our weaknesses and how it applies to this situation (2 Cor 12:9). _____

_____

_____

22.	Do you have a positive or negative attitude in and about this situation? Explain.

_____

_____

_____

Chapter 13
Fair Fighting Rules

1. Read chapter.
2. Fill out worksheet #5.
3. Fill out worksheet #19

Chapter 13
Worksheet #19
Fair Fighting Rules

Using this form develop your own set of Fair Fighting Rules to use with someone you are in a relationship with. Describe in detail why you choose each rule, why it is important, and how it will help your relationship. Try to develop several additional rules other than the ones mentioned in the text.

Who _____

What is the relationship? (i.e. mother/daughter, boyfriend/girlfriend, husband/wife).

_____

Rules:

1. _____

   _____

   _____

2. _____

   _____

   _____

   _____

3. _____

   _____

   _____

   _____

4. _____

   _____

   _____

   _____

5. _____

_____

_____

_____

6. _____

_____

_____

_____

7. _____

_____

_____

8. _____

_____

_____

_____

9. _____

_____

_____

10. _____

_____

_____

_____

Chapter 14
Parenting and Anger

1. Read chapter.
2. Fill out worksheet #5.
3. Develop your own chore and/or rule chart. Use the one at the bottom of this page for an example.
4. Fill out worksheet #20.
5. Do some research in your area to find as many agencies as you can that offer parenting classes, then compare them. Maybe even enroll in one. Go to the library and/or bookstore and look over the parenting books they have to offer. Buy or check out one to read.

Rules Chart							
	Mon	Tues	Wed	Thurs	Fri	Sat	Sun
No running, bouncing balls, or screaming in house.							
Do not go outside when parents are not home.							
No friends in house when parents are not home.							
Homework to be done before 5:00							
No video before homework							
No TV before homework							
No clothing items on floor							
No fighting with brother							
Rinse sink after brushing teeth.							
Totals							

Each time you break a rule you get 10 points. If you have above 100 points at the end of the week you will not get to play your video game for one week. If you have under 100 points you will get to pick out a video game to rent.

Chapter 14
Parenting and Anger
Worksheet #20

1. Describe any training you have had to be a parent. If you haven't had any outside training, the only other is what you experienced from the people who parented you. _____

   _____

   _____

   _____

   _____

   _____

2. What type of things have you heard about parenting from professionals? (i.e. James Dobson, Gary Smiley, Dr. Spock) _____

   _____

   _____

3. How do you feel about what you have heard? _____

   _____

   _____

4. At what level are you in parenting now? (i.e. no kids, number of kids and ages, only nieces, nephews, neighbors, friends, babysitting) _____

   _____

5. How do you think you are doing so far? Explain. _____

   _____

   _____

6. Do you know anyone that you would rate as very good parents? Who and why?

_____

_____

_____

7. What would you do/ do you do that is like them? Why? _____

_____

_____

_____

8. What would you never do like them? Why? _____

_____

_____

_____

9. What is your typical way of punishment? _____

10. Do you think this is appropriate? Why or why not? _____

_____

_____

11. What are additional things can you try to do for punishment? _____

_____

12. Have you ever witnessed someone verbally or physically abusing a child? How did you feel watching this? _____

_____

_____

13. What is your opinion about yelling? _____

_____

_____

_____

Chapter 15
Time-Outs

1. Read chapter.
2. Fill out worksheet #5.
3. Fill out worksheet #21.
4. Make an index card with questions (a) through (j) from worksheet #21 written out on it for you to use during your time-outs to help your self-talk.
5. Make a list of things you can do for your time-outs. You can use the list in the book for ideas.

Chapter 15
Time-Outs
Worksheet #21

1.   What do you do to relax? _____

_____

2.   What are your anger triggers? _____

_____

_____

3.   When are you the most angry? _____

_____

4.   When are your weakest times? _____

_____

5.   What body changes do you go through when you become angry? _____

_____

6.   Who do you fight with the most? _____

_____

7.   What are some of the thoughts the enemy tries to put in your head when you are
     angry? _____

_____

_____

_____

8.   Is it difficult for you to apologize? Why or why not? _____

_____

_____

9.   Answer the following questions about the last fight you got into (or the last time
     you were really angry):

     a.   What was the root cause? _____

b.   What other emotions were present (or stuffed) _____

_____

c.   How did you/were you feeling? _____

_____

d.   Who is this person (the one you were angry with)? _____

e.   List some positive facts about this person. _____

_____

_____

_____

f.   What do you think their perspective of the situation was? _____

_____

_____

_____

_____

g.   What did the enemy say to you (thoughts)? _____

_____

_____

_____

h.   Was the problem solved? _____

i.   Why or why not, and how? _____

_____

_____

_____

j.   Do you think time-outs will work for you? Why or why not? _____

_____

_____

Additional Topics

1. Read chapter.
2. Fill out worksheet #5. Compare the first one to the last one.
3. Fill out worksheet #22.
4. Retake anger checklist. Compare the first one to the last one.

Additional Topics
Worksheet #22

For each of the additional topics mentioned in the book, write if and how they affect you and how you can work towards improvements in each area.

Manipulation _____

_____

_____

_____

Control (you) _____

_____

_____

_____

Control (someone else) _____

_____

_____

_____

Guilt _____

_____

_____

_____

The need to be right _____

_____

_____

_____

_____

Defensiveness _____

_____

_____

_____

Self-pity _____

_____

_____

_____

Trying to get attention _____

_____

_____

_____

Getting even _____

_____

_____

_____

Jealously or Envy_____

_____

_____

_____

Criticism _____

_____

_____

_____

Power _____

_____

_____

_____

Embarrassment_____

_____

_____

_____

Delays _____

_____

_____

_____

Other's ignorance_____

_____

_____

_____

_____

Humor _____

_____

_____

_____

_____

Channeling or redirecting anger_____

_____

_____

_____

_____

Writing letters and/or journaling _____

_____

_____

_____

_____

Drinking and/or drugs_____

_____

_____

_____

_____

Apologies_____

_____

_____

_____

_____

Domestic violence _____

_____

_____

_____

1. What have you learned about the choices you make when managing your anger?

_____

_____

_____

2. What anger triggers have you recognized and how has this helped you to manage your anger appropriately? _____

_____

_____

3. What root issues have you recognized which have caused you to become an angry person? _____

_____

_____

4. In the past, what emotions did you avoid expressing, displaying anger instead, and how have you learned to identify and express those emotions? _____

_____

_____

5. What is the root of your rejection issues and how have you learned to deal with those issues in appropriate ways? _____

_____

_____

6. In the past, how has negative, self-defeating thoughts played a part in how you have handled your anger? _____

_____

_____

7. How has positive self-talk helped you to overcome the negative, self-defeating thoughts? _____

_____

_____

8. How has your history played a part in the unrealistic expectations you have for yourself and others? _____

_____

_____

9. How have unrealistic expectations played a part in your anger at yourself and others? _____

_____

_____

10. Explain how you have learned to overcome the unrealistic expectations you have had for yourself and others. _____

_____

_____

11. How have previous life experiences helped form your perspective?_____

_____

_____

12. How does seeing another's (possible) perspective help you to adjust your level of anger when things don't go your way? _____

_____

_____

13. How have you changed the way you manage your anger as a result of this program? _____

_____

_____

15. What do you think was is the most effective tool you have learned during this program? _____

_____

_____

16. How do you plan to use this tool in the future? _____

_____

_____

17. How do you plan to continue your journey to appropriate anger management?

_____

_____

_____

_____

_____

Please email me at drteresadavis@cox.net **and let me know how this program has helped you learn to manage your anger. Please include personal testimonies. If you enjoyed the book/workbook, please log on to one or more of your favorite book retailers and write a review. Thank you. Dr T.**